I, Orange Girls:
See if the slut can catch

Also by Ralph-Michael Chiaia

Ten Poems about East Asia & Kitsch Nebula Ampersands And

For Monks Only

The Sacred Calendar

Glyphic

I, Orange Girls

Ralph-Michael Chiaia

<Ralph’s Bookstore>
<2013>

First Printing: 2013

ISBN <Enter your ISBN>

rmchiaia.com-

Contents

Acknowledgements

A few of these poems appeared in *Ink, Sweat, & Tears*, *Clockwise Cat*, and *Yellow Mama* for which grateful acknowledgement is made.

These poems were all written between 2007-2008

I, Orange Girls

1.
it's raining
out
I hear the sprinklers
machine gunning water

I'm back in the US
from Korea
with a pad
ready to recount my story
from abroad

2.
years ago I bought
a canopy bed
crafted wood
with horizontal bars
for curtains
Vietnamese Mahogany

they liberated all those people

from the Khmer Rouge
how bad can their bed be?
ancient patterns, hand-crafted wood
the people that built Angkor Wat
the Khmers, the Bayon
intricate carvings of the universe
of the soul, of the mind in solid wood
around the mattress

now mom's got K-mart modern, geometric
sheets on it
and it bugs the hell out of me!

3.
Since born I've been allergic to dogs
eyes swollen and red
tired, grumpy
heavily sedated with medicine.

I was always tired while growing
up
now I'm strong—once out of
the house I got healthy:
ate well, drank juice

conquered my
allergies.

I come here. Mom has bought
a dog.
I spend the night coughing and
rubbing my eyes. Now I'm
exhausted.

4.
my allergies had me
in a ball on the floor

the dog hair was everywhere

I was too weak to
get it off

let it fucking kill me!
let it fucking kill me!
let it fucking kill me!
dog dander, enemy of

the asthmatic

I am my own martyr!
take me! put me on
my own t-shirt
tattoo me on my own chest:
man who withstood allergies
man who died trying

5.
I don't want
to break up
I don't want
to stay
alone, the house is so clean
cause I'll miss her
together, the sex gets deep n heavy
I need a sign a synchronicity
cause she does my head in!

I miss the Jjii-gae
I miss the late night drinking
the free pool tables
the furtive glances from

girls on the arms of boyfriends

6.
I left Ana
because
I felt this
tension
up through my back

like she physically
made me
sick

exactly want I feel
now
with Jinx

is it that the girls are no good
or is that what a relationship
simply feels like?

7.

Perhaps, if you see enough
of any
single love

you'll learn to hate
their very guts

8.
All week has been
traffic
to Yeonhui and back

I was going about
150 km/h
when a drunk
swerved into me.

Korean crackhead didn't even know
he'd done anything improper.

9.
Koreans

get all burned up
offended

by things they misunderstand

but by nature, they misunderstand
a lot
since culturally they're so weak
with language and thinking

I suppose many would call
that stupid
but it isn't

here relationships are one-way
top-down, so rules
take heavier precedent
over thinking

interpretation and discourse is looked down
on

so the cool ones
the ones down the looking glass
are awesome, secure
fun,
but the others
are

10.
business men on the street
red-faced and screaming
like mad infants. they are drunk
on soju. one falls aleep
against the curb. I put
one 10,000 (Man) Won note next
to him. he wakes up and yells:
“I am a business executive! I
don’t need your money, you gorilla
foreigner!”
I leave the money there, saying:
“then act like a businessman.”
his face crinkles with confusion, honest
confusion, then he says: “but I am.”

11.
Pilsoo went to Hong Kong
where he learned to trade stocks
in the pit

learned in the London tradition
was a highly-touted young
investment banker

took a job in prestigious Yeouido, Seoul
but was fired immediately upon
suggesting using some London-based ideas

12.
I hate her
never want to see her again

yet she reads on my bed

I want to destroy everything
we've built
I yelled, "just go home!"

until she exploded—crying and
stomping her feet on the ground.
she looked herself in the room.
I went for a walk. now she's asleep
on the bed.

I hate her
never want to see her again

then her skirt gets my eyes
to dance down her leg

i hike it up
and hate her a little less

13.
The Korean channel
has some B class
modeling
on Dong Ah TV
Dong Ah, I don't
know what it means

Ank by
Miria Sabino
one letter
per name
from
the great
psychedelic master:

Maria Sabina

14.
my idiot students
think
no, that's not the word,
believe because they've
been told,
being a teacher
is better
than being a writer

they have no idea the infinite success
it is

to be even a slightly-exposed artist.

15.
I’m surrounded by
idiot optimists
cynical is the only

way to be.
Mom says she
misses someone

saying, “I love you.”
I told her
they’re always lying

she laughed her optimism
clear off.

16.
Some half-wit
dude up the street
tried to save face

once
so he murdered
his girlfriend
cause she accepted
his
ding-a-ling
wouldn't work right.

17.
Driving 150 km/h
last night
through Seoul,
I braked
to a near-stop
merged left
saw right:
a shirtless man
on the pavement
another standing
over him.
I can understand
being drunk and
getting naked
I can understand
fighting

but get off the highway!

18.
thanks to Alison Ross

melting clock morning
says Salvador Dalai Llama
my legs are spindly
“like stilts,” says the llama
I walk a
desert-scape
while tigers bounce out
of pomegranates
with bayonets
pointed at Venus
that ancient Jinx
she’s asleep, naked
I just
planted pomegranate
seeds in her
then turned to a llama
and said, “I wish, furry dude.”
I ponder the meaning

of this
until a bee stings
me: a pomegranate stinger

19.
I keep a basket of oranges
in the car.
every time I see a really hot girl
I mean disgustingly hot
the kind that makes you involuntarily
moan,
I throw one at her

20.
there's this Japanese, or is it
Korean, custom
that if you catch an orange
you're accepting marriage

not that I want to marry
a disgustingly hot girl—gotta
be crazy to—it's more like
I'd just like an hour or two

21.
47 oranges have hit the pavement
this decade, 3 remain in the basket.

knee high socks and a plaid skirt, mmnnn—
I hope the slut can catch.

22.
these rich kids
drive foreign cars
around Apgujeong
and shout *ya-ta*
when they see a hot one
"you, get in!" girls, hot ones,
get in—

what kind of girl thinks she
should do this?

after a rough blow job Ji-hyun
gets dropped off on some side street

she wanted to be one of those
hot, desired girls—the rich ones

they are the ones driving the cars.

23.
I ate at 9:30 p.m. again
my mind it is a Martian
tightrope mindwalker

the sound of pressing an old
computer keyboard
the old-fashioned blip

my cock is a picture frame
a momento
a souvenir
a vibrating bunny

24.

All women are whores
he pushed my
head down
I was trembling
and tight
I couldn’t relax my mouth
enough to take it

it made me vomit
he threw me out of his car

25.
I can’t get off
at that station
the people mover
is under fluorescent
bulbs, the
floor is mirrored
it’s like a fractal
a panic fractal
my mind won’t handle it

then don’t meet me
she says

she hangs up

I'm handicapped
so arbitrarily
seized by terror.

26.
She's yelling at me again
I'm telling her she didn't
do anything wrong
she hears that I'm calling her
irrational
these arguments are lose-lose for me
she gets angry if I yell
angry if I'm calm
she stomps over and smacks my shoulder

I'm cutting a red pepper
I watch the knife

I watch the knife

27.
is there anything wrong
with
sleeping around?

Sophia, Cindy, Cecilia, Yeji
it's like a Beatles song

it's almost 3 a.m.

this carb-depletion I've tried
has my mind
pumped full of efficiency
I'm a salsa spin
a chipotle chili

an Arabian Mocha-Java
been-bean-bin

Bornea and Brunei. The Sultan.

28.
Cambodia, 1973
B-52 bombers have started
carpet bombing the Eastern
half of the country. this makes
bringing recruits into the Khmer
Rouge that much easier.

today's bombings of Iraq and
Afghanistan make bringing
recruits into the Islamists
that much easier.

29.
she reads a lonely planet
guide to Cambodia on
the bed. all you have to do
is read one of these to see
that today's policies are
absolute dog crap.

30.

a.
seeing my poems in print
again
my cock is hard
—so
distracting—it's a sine and cosine
a moth-sings opera
as water is lifting
weights. it prepares for twelve rounds
with that bad ass dust mite

green and red fractals hover over lakes and
rivers
pop songs have 128 tracks
blended—post-
ancientism = coatlism
I promised I'd write something
meaningful but my cock is up
I'm hungry, and my eyes are
itchy
—who could get
all the rebellions
to put down their
weapons
their holy books
their registers

and manifestoes?
when still

there's no food on the table
no clean running water

b.
the urn says it's about truth
beauty
peace.

c.
the net says it's about money
power
sex.

d.
it, the urn maybe, has shattered into a
million eyes
a million suns
it has reflected
like a shaved head

it's deep in prayer
nose up
knickers down

palms up
guns down

e.
it's yer birthday! it's yer birthday!
say kid, i guess I'll have another
cigarette

31.

1.
she stares
I wave
she scowls
I stare

2.
she stares
I scowl
she watches
I ignore

3.
she stares
I stare
she smiles
I smile

4.
she wipes
I dress
the door
it opens

5.
it slams
I leave
she waits

I wait

6.
she broods
I wait
she plots
I flee

32.
Aren't you glad
you

never married me?

of course, I'd screw around on

you her

too next

I like every shape
size
taste.

period

33.
I fast-walk the street
check my phone
send a message

I fast-walk
cause I have to get
to the bar

I have to
now

I can still feel her breath on
the wind will blow it off
me—

I have to
fast-walk

34.
In the jungle there
the lacandon
fire-eaters
jugglers
unicyclists
taught me

I need water, water
please

I walk into the jungle
past glow-worms
on trees

to vomit
there are chickens
of all things

just clucking around

35.
read me
buy my books:
anthologize me, publish me
snap me, blog me, upload
me
me
me me me
google me, dogpile me
index me, bookmark me
tumble me,
re-blog m4,
rss me,
cauterize me, anesthetize me
come hard and
fuck me

36.
she climbed up the bar
jumped up
grabbed a light

then dove on the ground

the EMTs said she OD'd

when I took my shoes off
later, a needle was sticking out
injected in the sole
I trembled removing the
shoe—found it hadn't punctured
any skin.

37.
I'm in the park again.
I dangle myself at her
"it's so big," she says
and purrs
stone tigers roar
"you're disgusting," she says
with myself growing in her hand,
"all you want is to finish."
then her throat muscles are a ring
that won't come off a finger dying
to get wed. she wants to get wed
so she sucks and sucks

in this dark park, hearing footsteps
I hold her head
I push it down I push it down
in the distance the old drunks, the
kids, the families. her slightest,
most miniscule movements coax
cream from me
into her, she grunts this guttural kind of
caterwaul, a kind of guggle,
her eyes go real wide, but it's not
cause of my meat. it's from the cum
hot down the back of her tongue
into her throat
from the eyes on her, her the slut,
her the slag, but it's dark, it's hard
to tell. we freeze like that.
an old man walks by, he wears
a hat that's too big with a military insignia
on the front that I see when he looks
he may think I'm holding
a girl who just failed a test, letting her cry,
or think she just broke up with
a boyfriend. or he may think
I'm letting the slut's
palatine tonsils milk out the last drop of
my cumshot. I don't really care.

38.
‘m sick of this but here I am again
girlfriend on the couch, TV blabbing
about style or style icons or some shit
paris hilton’s shadow is dancing the back
wall--
as the papparrazzis pop and crackle away--
like a coked up popper or LSD-laced raver
as she pulls her torso back from her hips
and smiles—just like taught in some weird
finishing school—as the paparazzi continue
making that shadow dance.

39.
I’m leaving the stem in my poems.
I don’t think Robert Hass wrote poems
about skullfucking and such. I will
never be a poet with this mind. I need
to cut it out, like the way you remove
the seeds and stem when slicing an apple.
Nobody wants to eat the stem!

40.

I don't need a soul mate, baby
I need a hole mate, baby
get on fours like a beast
the Kama Sutra
calls this Congress of the Cow, baby

41.
Today I Had to change a Tire Blowout
some idiot came forward at my car
while I was pulled over and nyquil'd
I hit some metal rods lying on the ground
pop.

42.
my throat is itchy
friday's drinks may have
gotten me

43.
my throat is itchy
sunday's drinks may have
gotten me

44.
my throat is itchy
all that talk
to get her to come home with me
may have gotten me

then after I got her
I didn't even want her

45.
it's like a curtain closing,
all wrinkles, red, and slightly uneven
you see feet running around underneath.
it's like an electric eye closing
like maniacal laughter
like the smell of ammonia as the bartender mops
you lounge, a pretty French girl, peers at you
like grapes hanging from a tree.
you lounge, a young Korean girl you are ass-fucking on Fridays
sits across from you while her best friend
lays across your chest.
that smell is getting too strong. you tap her

get up, and finish of your vodka.
it’s closing time.
you knew that.

About the Author

Ralph-Michael Chiaia likes playing with toy trains. He was born next to the biggest landfill in the world. Now he lives in a city that can be easily mistaken for a garbage dump. Luckily he has a beautiful family with a two-year-old son who also likes playing with toy trains.

Find more about him at his junky looking official site rmchiaia.com or check out his blog at ralphadelic.blogspot.com

If you liked these poems, please leave a review wherever you acquired it.

www.ingramcontent.com/pod-product-compliance
Ingram Content Group UK Ltd.
Pitfield, Milton Keynes, MK11 3LW, UK
UKHW020215250726
13967UKWH00001B/10

9 781304 637680